A

POET'S

JOURNEY

Inspirational Poetry by:

WORD WARRIOR

A POET'S JOURNEY

Printed in the United States of America

ISBN-13:978-0692425213
ISBN-10:0692425217

Printed by Createspace 2015

Published by BlaqRayn Publishing Plus 2015

Typist: LeShera Beatty

<u>Dedication</u>

I WOULD LIKE TO DEDICATE MY FIRST BOOK OF POETRY TO MY TWO AWESOME GRANDMOTHER:

HELEN K. FELTON AND GLADYS DICKEY

FOR THEIR PRAYERS AND CONSTANT DISCIPLINE AND KEEPING ME GROUNDED IN THE CHURCH! WITHOUT THEM I DON'T KNOW WHERE I WOULD BE TODAY! ! !

I LOVE Y'ALL ~ GRANDMA & MAMA 4 LIFE!!!

R.I.P.

A

POET'S

JOURNEY

Inspirational Poetry by:

WORD WARRIOR

CHAPTER 1
"An AWESOME
"GOD"

"IT IS NO SECRET WHAT "GOD" CAN DO!!"

We have to remember "GOD" is the head of it all, he brings the summer, spring & fall. He wakes us up each and every day; he keeps us in his care while we're on our way. Follow the Ten Commandments that's what we're told to do. Give him a tenth of our earnings and we'll make it through. The Lord giveth and takes it away! Just trust in the Lord keeps your head high and prays. When you call on the Lord he might not come right away but he's always right on time they say! The Lord is in the blessing business I can testify, he is so good to me sometimes I have to cry, never be afraid to call on him even in the worst times, when the road looks dim. "when things get rough and you cannot see" father I stretch my hands to thee, "GIVE IT TO GOD" he'll work it out, no more worries and no more doubts, when the bills are high and the money is low and you really don't know which way to go! "Trust in the Lord he's the only way that we're going to make it in the world today." If you really don't know if you'll make it thru! "IT IS NO SECRET WHAT GOD CAN DO!"

"BLESSED & HIGHLY FAVORED"

Where do I start? How do I even begin? About how good god has been to me until there is no end.

Blessed meaning fortunate enjoying happiness or pleasure, another interpretation is gifted or many treasures.

Highly meaning relatively great advanced in development, up at the top or #1 the finest of the click.

Favored meaning privileged approval or support, pretty much creme of the crop & never the last resort.

If everyone has 3 angels of guidance 2 watch over them, I truly believe I had 10 especially when out on a limb.

When times got very difficult& extremely complicated, I dropped 2 my knees & bared the storm because without god I wouldn't of made it.

For some reason I draw drama, even with women & throughout life, I guess because I was so grounded the Lord held me super- Tight!

There is truth in the saying god doesn't give you more than you can bear, because even in my most intensive moments I knew that he was there!

Through all my turmoil and struggles through life, when things got severe and I could not fight, He's Alpha & Omega he rolled me through god is so amazing I thought you knew.

God is so real, I want you 2 know, he is not a myth, game or show, he's always been official from a child 2 a man, I've always been blessed & highly favored, I guess that's in his plan.

I want to thank the god above for giving me so much beautiful love.

If my life ended now & I could not breathe, I know there's a special place in heaven 4 me!

REPENTANCE

There comes a time, when you're tired of your road being rough, when you're at the end and you're all fed up.

When you tell yourself, that's enough of doing wrong, no more darkness it's been too long.

I'm really ready to change my life, no more heartache & 2 much Strife.

The road of wrong has gone on too long, I'm going to completely surrender and keep my faith strong.

I finally realized where my effort & majority of time was being spent; now I'm ready, willing & able to repent.

It's not going to be easy but with god, strong will and determination, keeping yourself focused you'll have a better situation.

There's good & evil, which one will you choose, pick the right one or you're going to lose.

Life can be interesting depending on which way you make your bed, or maybe it's the way you lay, at the foot or the head.

With god there's no half-stepping, or faking the funk, because once you chose him, you choose the right one.

If you think your life has been navigating in the wrong direction, make a right down the Lords street you'll find love & affection.

If you're searching for a peace of mind, no further looking just give him some time, if you're seriously & sincerely about changing your ways, first step to beginning is just starting to pray.

"GOD IS GOOD ALL THE TIME"

For every action, there's a reaction, a reason 4 everything we do, but there comes a time when we wonder why is this happening 2 u?

Sometimes were being tested, 2 c how well we can endure, 2 find out if our faith is weak or is it really pure?

Once you come to the point, that you will not complain, & you know god is good & he will never change.

You'll find a peace of mind, that's joyful & full of life, its nothing left but 2 thank him, night after night.

Thank you Lord for keeping me safe, thank you Lord 4 having your way, thank you Lord 4 everything that you do, thank you Lord 4 all I've been thru.

You've brought me thru problems, when I couldn't find away 2 solve them, you brought me through my troubles, all my heartache & my struggle.

Have you ever felt like you were stuck somewhere, no motion at all, no one 2 turn 2, no one 2 hear your call?

No matter which way you turned, you could not get out? No one to hear your scream no one to hear your shout?

When you feel like this & start going out of your mind, call on god, he's good all the time

<u>PRAYER CHANGES THINGS</u>

If you ever had a problem that picked your mind like you do collard greens, then you don't know the power & change that prayer brings?

When there's a heavy burden that's got you all-depressed & worn out, just give it to god& he will work it out!

When your way is so dark, you cannot see the light just pray 2 the Lord consistently night after night!

If there's a chance of divorce between you & your spouse when you're behind on the mortgage & might lose the house, your teenage daughter might be with child & the boss is saying there going to lay you off for a while.

There is a man upstairs, who receives what you bear, and you can lay them on his chest & put your mind to rest! When the problems are eating at your brain & troubling your brain & troubling your heart once you give it to god hell tear it apart!

I really don't know what else to tell you except the god will not fail you! If you have any type of care you better give it to god in prayer!

<u>GRACE</u>

As a child, you learn grace young, still getting treats & love even though your chores weren't done.

As you mature & increase with age, you still encounter grace, through life different phases.

All through life you come across people who don't deserve your grace, but you manage to distribute it anyway.

People will try to take advantage of your grace, no matter what gender, age or even the race, their raw concentrated & hard like alcohol with no chase.

There are some people that are hard, cruel & cold; they will attack at your grace every which way they know.

I would like to touch on god's grace that is out of this world that is given to every man woman, boy & girl.

Even through our failures, mistakes & heartaches, we still receive his favor, day after day.

It was pre-meditated when he died for our sins; he hung on the cross so we can be born again.

Praises go up & blessings come down, that's just another sign of grace just hitting the ground.

There's no other way & no need to look, god's grace is phenomenal even when you are booked.

"THE DEVIL IS A LIAR"

The devil is a liar, I want you 2 know, if it wasn't true I wouldn't tell you so, he attacks your mind & craves your soul & will not stop until he has control.

He likes to invade your peace, & conquer your joy, his main 3 goals are kill, steal & destroy. Please don't give into these demonic ways because once he gets you you're in his maze.

A just man falls 7 times & gets back up, this anger the devil when a man of god stands up! He makes things look good that really are not, & he is overwhelmed when chaos & destruction hits the block.

He can make married men cheat, even temp a pastor to creep; he will turn a son against his mother, &will have a man loving another.

He's #1 when it comes to temptation; he used to be an angel that's why he has so much frustration. Please believe me the devils a liar if you're under his wing you'll endure eternal fire.

"? FORGIVE ME LORD?"

Forgive me Lord, for all the times I've been wrong, forgive me Lord for not being strong, I'm sorry Lord for not giving you enough time in my life, I'm sorry Lord just for not acting right, forgive me Lord, for not being a better father to my kids forgive me Lord for all the bogus things I've did. Forgive me Lord for not being abundant to you; forgive me Lord for not seeing things thru. Forgive me Lord for not obeying the law; forgive me Lord for everything that's my fault. Forgive me Lord for choosing to do things my way, I am so thankful & humble for your love, mercy &amazing grace,

Forgive me Lord, I just want to do better, I'm ready to receive you Lord now & forever.

Forgive me Lord what else can I say? Please give me your forgiveness Lord & just have your way.

"TRUST HIM"

Trust him with your worries, trust him with your doubts, trust him with your insecurities trust him with all your thoughts.

Trust him with your issues, trust him with your pain, and trust the Lord with everything & nothing will remain.

Trust him with your cravings, trust him with your lust, trust him with your weakness, and trust him with your guts.

Trust him with your hopes, trust him with your dreams, trust him with your secrets, and trust him with everything.

If you're wondering if you're on the right road, once you given it 2 him, only miracles will unfold.

Intensive moments, crucial points, times of duress, boiling points, life. Changing decisions, voting & honorable mention.

IN ALL THESE THINGS, NO WORRY OR FUSS "IN GOD WE TRUST"

"ALL YOU NEED"

If you need a friend, he's all you need, if you need instructions open his word & read.

If you need guidance he is the light, if you need understanding he'll get you right.

If you're lacking love, he's there for you, because of his grace you'll make it through.

If you need motivation as we usually do, he'll uplift your spirits I thought you knew.

If you need a doctor, & you're below the weather just call on the Lord he'll get you together.

If you need an attorney in your court case, invite his presence and he want be late.

Whatever you ask? It will be given to you, blessings overflowing through & through.

Whatever you need just send up the prayer, believe it or not it's already there.

If you need a spouse & you're sincere at heart, he'll send you someone & you'll never part.

If you need finance for any situation, just trust& believe & you'll realize he is the greatest.

Times of duress, what do I do? Times of trouble can I make it through? I might be homeless where am I going to go?

God is all you need I want you to know!

"GOT GOD"

There comes a time when you overlook your life & you start to wonder if you're wrong or right? If god is in your spirit, soul & mind. Nine times out of ten you'll be just fine.

God has to be in your spirit, he has to be in your walk god has to be in your heart he has to be in your talk. He has 2 be in your life no second guessing once you're submitted to him they'll be nothing but blessings.

Someone may ask you are god real? There's an overwhelming joy that you start to feel! It's called peace, it comes from above- this beautiful peace is his forgiving love! Anything you want just simply ask? Anything you want- just simply ask? Anything you need he's up to the task. He'll make your darkness turn 2 lights. Praise the Lord he's in my life!

"KEEP PRAYING"

Take it to god if it's troubling your mind, take it 2 gods, and give him some time. Come from your heart just keep it real, sugar-coat nothing let him know how you feel.

It may be something sensitive, or even deeply profound, it really doesn't matter because he will work it out. There's noting too big, or even to small any type of issue he handles it all.

Send it to god with no hesitation, it will stop any defeat, pain or frustration, in order for your prayer to work you must have faith & keep praying until it hurts. Delay is not denial, so please don't stop. We have 2 pray continuously 4 the blessing to drop.

God will give you the desires of your heart; as long as you take it to him in prayer you've made your start. Faith, belief & continuous prayer if all done correctly you want have a care.

"THANK YOU"

Thank you for my good days & I also thank you 4 the bad.

Thank you for my happy moments & I even thank you for the sad.

I appreciate you Lord, for teaching me through all situations, for educating me with your word & blessing me with patience.

Thank you Lord 4 everything that you've done, thank you Lord 4 sending your son, thank you Lord 4 remaining true, without you Lord what would I do?

When my night is cold, you are my heat you've warmed my body from head 2 feet! When my way is dark, you are my light, your love 4 me is out of sight.

There is no one that could take your place, forgiving love day after day, when I'm wondering how I'm going 2 eat my stomach get filled without defeat.

When my days are rainy, you are the sun, thank you Lord because you are the one.

From waking me up 2 keeping me safe at night, thank you for my gift of being able 2 write!

"DECISIONS"

As I sit here, pondering in receiving at this Shawnee joint, let me stop playing with my thoughts& get to the point.

There are some hard decisions that I'm going to have to make, so I won't ever have to return to god, a degrading place.

Decision- meaning decide, choose, choice, or selection, picking the right road staying legit in the right direction.

It's really not hard, pretty simple if you ask, it's like two plus two and it's pretty much simple math.

Yes I'm a hustler, that is the slang name, but really I'm a networker, & an asset to any game having the ability to make ends meet, having the ability to survive in the streets blessed with a gift of communication, blessed with a gift of transporting information.

Once I put it all together, I will figure it out, because the bills will still be there & that's without a doubt.

Decisions are a major part of life, there's selection in everything we do, there are multiple choice, right & wrong which one will you choose?

"AT PEACE"

When mind boggling issues have left your brain, when earth shuttering news drop & you stay sane!

When things don't upset you like they usually do, & you realize all worrying and nervousness is through.

No matter how your day goes, you just smile & receive it, because you do not complain you're at peace & believe it!

It's a calmness you feel, it runs from your head 2 your heart, it's like things are all good it's like making a new start.

There are so many things that can raise your blood pressure, extraordinary things where you just cannot measure.

An issue with you child, a problem with your mat, something serious with your spouse, we all can relate.

My definition of peace is relaxed, & anxiety free, all my thanks go to god for blessing me with peace!

"HOW EXCELLENT"

If you're looking for a miracle, & expect the impossible
there's a GOD that's willing and able.

At times we become depressed, when our outcome wasn't
the best, even though we still did well & we truly excelled,
but in our heart& mind we failed.

There is a god who will pick you up, Turn you around,
place your feet on solid ground, correct your thoughts
change your ways, & you'll only see brighter days.

You send him your prayer, with belief; it stops the sadness
& the grief. He answers it when he's ready too, now thank
you Lord you made it through.

If you're wondering if you're going 2 make it, when it's
time to take the test & you don't want 2 take it!

When all life's issues have got you down, when you want 2
smiles, but can only frown.

You must know that there is a man, who has the world in
his hands who picks us up when we've fall short I tell you
one thing he's my first resort!

God is good, god is great, and there is no risk that I
wouldn't take. Knowing that he has my back, there is
nothing I will not lack!

Knowing & asking what he has 4 me, I should turn out
excellent as can be!

When my rides been rough, where I could not bear, even through the bumps I knew that he was there.

When I thought that I was in the belly of the whale, god brought me through the storm so I could prevail!

He's past good; he's exceeded great, excellence you'll have if you have his grace!

"KEEP ME STRONG LORD"

Keep me strong Lord, in my daily walk, strengthen me Lord even in my talk.

Keep me strong Lord as I stroll through life; give me guidance & direction as I look for a wife.

Strengthen me Lord when I'm feeling weak, guide my thoughts before I speak, keep my mind stead on you, I'm so thankful you're in my life, I just don't know what to do.

Where do I go from here? What do I do next? I know you got me Lord, because you are the best.

I wouldn't have made it this far, without you, thank you Lord, you are the truth.

I'm asking for strength, courage, patience & love & I know it's already granted because it's from above.

Give me strength as I make decisions, keep me strong as I handle my business, make me over, make me better, stay with me Lord now & forever.

You are my strength, you are the head of my life, you are my rock, and you are my light.

Thank you for my strength, thank you for your power, thank you for your grace

EACH & EVERY HOUR.

"LET GO & LET GOD"

Release the problem, losing your grip, the hold you had let it slip. Send it up with belief; get rid of it, just like a thief.

Let it go without a care, what you're asking is always there!

He will not give you more than you can manage, so releasing it to him is to your advantage.

He's the only one you need to turn to, god is magnificent he makes it do what it do.

Even though your flesh is hostile towards him, your faith will endure & you've surpass the dim.

Give god the glory; give god the praise, not just when you're worried but each & every day.

God is the answer, I really want you 2 know, take it to the alter & just simply let it go!

"GOD~CRAZY"

Father- god I love you so much, when your spirit hits me
my soul tingles, I know it's your touch.

Eight out of ten things I ask, I receive I guess because I'm
faithful & obedient & I do believe.

I'm so thankful for this intimate & personal relationship
with you; without you Lord I couldn't have made it through.

In times of trouble, you are there, in times of nervousness, I
know you care, in times of sadness you make me smile, and
I am so thankful that I'm your child.

All things are possible only thru you; I am god crazy I
thought you knew!

Thank you Lord for everything, thank you Lord for
blessing me. Thank you Lord for being the head of my life,
I am god crazy until I die!

"FAITH"

Faith is belief turned inside out; as long as you believe you kill all doubt!

Knowing that you will achieve, only because you truly believe.

Name it, then claim it, and after you win you can frame it!

Walk in the room with a clear mind, knowing that you're going 2 win inside.

When the demons attack you, the angels are fierce at hand; ready 4 battle on your demand.

It all starts with the thought process, faith & belief equals success!

Knowing that you'll win the race, knowing that you'll beat your case, knowing that you'll pass the test, knowing that you are the best!

Something's are just a test of faith, 2 see how long u can endure the race!

Faith is measured by what you put in, knowing the outcome at the end.

When the flesh gets weak & the devil slips through just tell the devil what god can do!

When you're at the of your rope, don't give up & don't lose hope!

Tie a knot & hang on tight; knowing with god you'll be alright!

"I WONT COMPLAIN"

Sometimes things get hectic and your brain starts to frustrate, and you really have hard decisions 2 make.

Which bills 2 pay first, the kids need different things just dealing with life and the problems is brings.

Every problem must have a solution, but complaining about it just draws confusion.

Car note, insurance, is my working in vain? After you pay one bill, they keep falling like rain.

Somewhat stressed out one of the kids has gotten in trouble at school, now there calling me at work, and the boss is giving me the blues.

Once I get home the garage door won't open up, upon further investigation I realized someone has stolen my stuff!

At the end of my day, I go in my room & drop 2 my knees and give it 2 gods he's the only one who can give me peace!

After my prayer, I realize there's nothing ill change I have gave it 2 gods so "I will not complain."

"NOT ENOUGH FAITH"

From a child to a boy pretty much raised in church learned about god at a young age for all that its worth.

All through my adolescence

Bounce around threw a couple of religions but pretty much stay focused on god to my recognition.

Fell off from church just a little bit, but once my road got distorted, I was back at church in cinch.

I've had some dramatic episodes, and some near death experiences, so I know god is real, and he handles his business.

I've been blessed and highly favored all through my life, even caught a decent settlement, and still waiting on my wife.

Looked up and caught three cases, all of them at once, my father is this real been sitting in county for two months.

My faith is strong, and Lord knows I believe, but long as I am human and flesh I have to drop back to my knees.

Two inches of doubt, the devil steps right in, and I have to reinforce my faith again.

If the devil gets two inches, please believe he'll take a mile, next thing you know negativity is sitting for a while.

Is this me? With unbelief, thinking he'll leave me alone?
Thank you Lord, thank you Lord now my faith is back and
strong!!

CHAPTER 2

INCARCERATION

"INCARCERATION"

Just take a moment, a few minutes of your time, & we'll dig down deep inside the mind of an incarcerated bro that's doing time.

Imagination running crazy, heavy thoughts that come from glazing, wondering what's going on in the other world, away from your kids and your girl.

They've locked up my body, & took my rights; they've taking control of my life.

I'm somewhere in here behind these walls; these fools even regulate my phone calls.

I took for granted what I used to do. If I could do it all over, I would reverse the truth.

They can incarcerate my flesh & try to manipulate my mind, but they cannot kill my character &pride.

If its rehabilitation that they're looking 4, yes I've endured it, and that's 4 sure.

I dint think you ever had a vivid enough imagination, to create the thoughts of incarceration in order to be here there must be some criminal participation but not a high level of education.

Malcom X, Martin Luther King, Muhammad Ali, were locked up, and then became free. I guess there no prejudice that's behind bars from the average Jew to mega stars.

Keep your mind tuned to the right stations, stay out of the
wrong locations, & you'll probably escape
"INCARCERATION"

"JUDICIAL SYSTEM"

Such an interesting title, so I decided to write listening to these bros outcomes of cases night after night.

I should of followed my first mind & became an attorney years ago because I would of went that route, I would have been better off for show!

During my stay at cook county jail, I researched the law library a lot, and tried 2 find a way 2 get bail! This judicial system is so bogus, ill & corrupt; it's full of so much BS &just the opposite of justice.

But I come to find there's honor & favor to paid attorneys, and if you're blessed to have one you'll have a much smoother journey.

With a private attorney you can make power moves, from copping out, 2 large bond reductions to alternative program its true.

It goes like this, a paid attorney makes the move, the judge honors his word because he went to school; the court honors you because you have a mouth piece, next thing you know you're back on the streets.

The judicial system can blow your mind, but without that right counsel you can increase your time.

Anyone involved in criminal participation, please put some money 2 side for proper legal representation.

"REALITY OF CRIME"

If you have guts to does your crime, than you should have
the guts to do your time. You commit the crime with all
hands in; you commit the crime just doing what you did.
Once you got locked up & you're behind bars, that's when
all the second guessing & reminiscing starts.

I should have done it this way, I could've turned another
way but the truth of the matter is crime doesn't pay! We get
caught up in what were ding going hard day & night, so
you start to feel invincible & forget that it's not right,
locked up looking at four walls & then pressure starts to
fall, the silence can drive a sane person out of their mind,
but toughen up its called time.

Daylight come& you want to go home, daylight come and
you want to use the phone, daylight come and you wish you
wasn't here, daylight come now u got to face the fears. I'm
locked up, they won't let me out, I'm locked up does
anyone hear me scream & shout? I'm locked up I realized I
committed this crime! Let me stop relax & finish this time.

"RELEASE ME"

Do I act like a criminal? I'm just a man trying 2 eat, just trying 2 feed my family & survive in these streets.

Do I look like a criminal? Driving livery cab every day, don't be upset I just did it my way!

Do I seem like a criminal? Selling my customers movies, CDs & squares, making something out of nothing this just isn't fair.

A criminal is someone who breaks the law; I'm just a man that's maintaining so that means it's my fault.

I have five children that I planted their seed, so I work very hard trying 2 satisfy all their needs.

Between bills & the kids I'm pretty much a workaholic no doubt, father if you can hear me "PLEASE LET ME OUT."

I think I work so hard because I like the finer things, like Pelle Pell, big rims, & all the beautiful things that like can bring.

So does it make me a criminal because I work hard & like nice things in my book I don't think so so please release me?!

"FREE A SLAVE"

Am I a slave to this place? Am I a slave to this institution? Am I a slave to this jail? I wonder when they will lose me.

After so long, I mean once you acquired sometime, you sort of start to feel captive & even start to lose your pride.

First your freedom is gone, & you realized they've taken your rights; you can feel less of a man & want to give up the fight.

They throw you on a deck, & always interrupting your rest, who cares him just an inmate, if you don't like it bond out of this place.

It's cool I guess, I put myself here, I won't ever give these people my time, it's been a hell of a year.

You're stripped of your family; I mean everything that you loved; now I know how the hand feels when it's inside the glove.

Its real, I'm here I thought it was all a dream, it's been truly an experience & I know what jail means.

If you pass life test you'll find love & success, & if you fail you may experience being a slave at cook county jail!

"NO DISCRIMINATION"

Where do I start? How do I begin? About this no discrimination until there is an end.

Upon my stay at cook county jail, I realized, they do not discriminate on who they jail, from ages 17 to 78 they will accept all that comes through the gate.

People with psych issues, men that's out of their mind, bros missing limbs, they even take the blind.

No discrimination is their golden rule, if you commit a crime; they have a place for you.

Men with epilepsy, men that are paraplegics, even men with stage 4 cancer, with there are no further treatment.

They even have diabetes, don't worry they have paramedics, there pretty much prepared to deal with all endeavors.

You'll find men that are called to preach you'll find homosexuals that are sweet, you'll find artist & poets like me, and you even get bros that like 2 raise hell.

Take are men from all walks of life, you even got men who are strife, and there are bros that are corrupt & even men that have not grown up.

Do you think they discriminate? All religions and nationalities are in this place.

When I thought I seen it all & all of the varieties were through, oh yeah I forgot they even lock up the deaf &mute.

14,000 inmates & there's a female section too, cook county doesn't discriminate & by the way there building a new building too!

"HOW LONG"

How long is my suffering? How long will I fight? How long will it take 2 find out if I'm wrong or right?

How long will I be stressed? How long will I not eat correct? How long will god make me endure my vicious test?

How long will this go on? How long can I hold on? How long will I be weak? How long will I be strong?

How long will I hold up? How long before I fold up? How long is my punishment? How long before I grow up?

How long will I miss my family? How long will I miss my friends? How long will I be locked up? When will this madness end?

Continuance upon continuance to me meaning forever and so long. How long will it be before I make it home?

How long?

How long?

"STARTING OVER"

Sitting back just reflecting, pretty much trying to regroup, pushing away the old & coming with the new.

Do I pick up where I left off, or do I find something fresh? Whatever I do I have to endure life's test.

The old cliche is to change people, places & things, my choice is to be ready for whatever life brings.

Re-enter, re-learn, re-institute, return, I'm back, I'm here, I'm home, don't fear, once again don't hate it's me it's my day.

I'm in it, to win it, you can hate it or friend it, back to the grind, because I got to get mine.

It was short it wasn't long, I praise god I made it, what's up? What you on, trying to figure it out, I just got home.

Where do I go? Which direction will I start? Got to get it in order, it's time to do my part.

I think I'll change some of the things that I use to do, I'll drop some old friends & make some new.

I'm ready to start over; I can endure my change, time to do things different.

Time to make that change!

"THE PENAL SYSTEM"

Is this system really working? Because all institutions are filled to the max, system is so overcrowded everyone's praying good times comes back.

Is it the police, or the criminal who do you point the finger? All I know is there is a serious problem in these streets we need 2 find a solution 2!

I guess it's the economy, because there are no jobs, I guess that's why so many are committing crimes because times are so very hard.

I believe every 5 out of 10, did not commit their crime, so you have 5 who did, 5 who didn't but they all end up inside.

Some who get rehabilitated, some who manage 2 stay within their ways, some who repent and won't ever see the system again throughout their days.

The system is made 2 correct you & lead you 2 take the right road, but if you stay in a life of crime how many times you return you'll never know.

Is the system a success or failure? Do you really want 2 know? Just ask yourself how many people been locked up that you know?

Did it change their life? Did they return again, or was it just multiple times until it was no end!

The penal system is bogus, distasteful & nothing 2 bring about, if you are or ever been locked up, you just really want to get out!

"EVERYDAY IS A CLOSER DAY TO FREEDOM"

As I come towards the end & my time is almost up, and I really feel like I've really grown up.

And time is moving at a really fast pace & my emotions are jumping all over the place.

I feel like I've matured, I feel like I've learned my lesson, I feel like this encounter has truly been a blessing.

What an experience, I will soon be released, my trial & test will be over & my life will be at peace.

Staring out the window, knowing it'll all be over soon, brighter days beautiful sun, light rays no more dark days no more gloom.

The sun comes up, the sun goes down, hours into weeks & I will touch down.

I was ripped from the world, I was torn away from my life, now return me, and detach me so I can live right.

I've been rehabilitated, I do stand corrected; now reinsert me into society so I can be respected.

Whatever my issues, whatever their reasons, all I know right now every day is a closer day to freedom.

"LIVING IN THE BATHROOM"

I guess this is what it boils down to, 4 walls & a toilet this is true.

A set of bunk beds, a window, table, shelves, mirror & sink that's pretty much your cell.

Living in the bathroom, is pretty much bogus & degrading. Only person to get upset with is you because this is the way I made it.

Living in a bathroom is no way amusing or pleasing; you just don't won't to ever return for no type of reason.

Living in a bathroom, makes you miss your freedom, reminiscing about the simple things in life, and now you understand all the wrongs &rights.

Compact, small, 5 shelves, 4 walls, 4 coat hangers, 3 lights this is what consist of your life.

The toilet is connected to the sink, which is only a few feet away from feet, 1 door, one cell, one's hell.

There's nothing comfortable about this place, just living in the bathroom every day, locked up so far away from home, thank god I'm short it won't be long.

"NRC"

I heard a lot about this place some true, some not. I guess it's just another phase you go through before you make it back 2 the block.

First of all the food is 100 times better than cook county jail, more seasoned, more variety I just got to keep it real.

You receive your calculation sheet which has your out date, so you're thinking about all your desires &choices you're going to make. Being stuck in a room 24/7 is really not that bad, as long as you have a cool cellie. You all can talk about things & dreams that you had.

Going outside for 4 hours once a week is decent, but I can't wait to get 2 my joint so I can have more movement & freedom. Minutes, hours, days ticking away, it won't be long until my out date!

"LOCKED UP"

Please let me help you understand, the mindset of a caged, deprived locked up man.

Trying to figure out what brought you here, within a blink of an eye, within a wink of a tear.

It all happened so fast, how did this come about? But yes I'm locked behind bars without a doubt!

Freedom gone, family gone, man all the numbers I know are in my cell phone! As I sit here & ponder with nothing but time & a whole lot of questions why? Why? Why?

Dealing with bros, hearing all types of cases, with a lot of different attitudes & a lot of new faces!

I always been the type to fall right in place, I guess u can say "I'M COVERED IN HIS GRACE"!

As I sat in silence, a voice came 2 me, it said change your ways & this won't have to be!

3 times in 8 months you have my full attention! I'm being obedient I'm going to listen!

"I'M EXCITED & ANXIOUS"

I'm excited & anxious to make it home, I'm excited & anxious I wonder how long?

I'm excited & anxious for my feet to touch the ground; I'm excited & anxious to be back around.

I'm excited & anxious to jump on my Facebook page, knowing that my 600 friends will all be amazed.

I'm excited & anxious to get back to the world, man I can't wait to see my kids & fuss at my girl.

I'm excited & anxious let me calm down &be still because this time I will appreciate my freedom & know that it's real.

I'm excited & anxious missing family & friends, only feeling this way because this time eventually must end.

I'm excited & anxious knowing they can't hold me forever, it would be nice 2 get out there & catch some of that beautiful weather.

Sometimes I sit & ponder & wonder how long? Calm down & relax my precious child you're on your way home!

"THE HOUSE OF PRAYER"

A whole lot of movement in & out but I met a lot of good brothers without a doubt!

The presence of god is definitely on this tier, & I thank the Lord for sending me here.

There's been a lot of quarrels, & a couple of fights, but god kept this deck blessed night after night.

This house is sacred; believe it or not, once god gave me my inspiration my writing of poems has not stopped.

I received my personal & intimate relationship with him, while being here, my time has been blessed & it's been a great year.

I've overcome fears & even learned how to fast; I know god's grace & mercy here will forever last!

My assignment from god is to live in him, believe, & capture more souls, so I'm going to be obedient until my days get old.

Thank you Lord for the love that is here, thank you Lord for deleting my fears, thank you Lord for taking away all my cares!

I AM SO THANKFUL

FOR THE HOUSE OF PRAYER!

"IN THE OVEN"

I'm being thoroughly rinsed through & through; seasoned & marinated even my walk is new.

Temperature set just right, I've even shed some pounds, I believe all will see my glow when I'm back around.

Sauteed with onions & spices different juices to give an exquisite taste, get ready society, because I'm on my way.

I'm in the oven, & it's been a while I'm almost done, but when I'm ready ill being scrumptious & they'll be enough for everyone.

I'm in the oven, got my thoughts in order, & came up with a legit plan. I've got my personal & intimate relationship with god & ready to be a stand up man.

I'm in the oven, & it's very hot in here, it's been a minute almost a year.

I needed this time to get myself right, I'm decent, I'm good never again in life.

I'm the main course, & I'm almost ready, their preparing the side dishes, Cole slaw & spaghetti.

A few minutes more & I'll be right out, some of the best meat you ever tasted, delicious without a doubt!

"I'M GLAD IT'S OVER"

The first step of this process I made it through, cook county jail, that part is over; I just don't know what to do. Don't get me wrong, my deck was all good, it was really great, and I was just so tired of enduring the same situation day after day. My spirit was strong but my flesh was weak, & my tolerance level had reached its peak.

I had one of the hardest judges in the county they say, so I really don't regret getting out of her way. I felt she was very unfair, & at times pretty mean, so I was very much fed up with all of these things. She denied me a bond, also denied house arrest, she pretty much denied every single one of my request. I beat one case in trial, & copped out the other two, my spirit was strong but my flesh was ready to be through. So I fasted & asked god to reveal it to me, should I stay & fight or cop out & later become free.

A scripture was brought to my attention. "If you can gain your freedom do so", also god spoke to me & my mind was made it was time to go. So I thank the Lord for revealing my decision to me, I'm sitting here writing this in my second phase.

NRC.

"TURNING NEGATIVE INTO POSITIVE"

During my stay at cook county jail, & after I realized they wouldn't give me bail, I sat & analyzed what god wanted from me, started my task of my new daily routine.

More praying & praying like never before, more reading of his word until my eyes got sore. Now having an intimate & personal relationship with him, now my days are bright & never are dim.

I have more knowledge of his word now than ever in life; the love of god is out of sight! I've lived 39 years & been through all type of situations but my true peace with the Lord, came through my **INCARCERATION**! I've been a member of six different churches, wow what the heck? Seen the most abundant blessing on my prayer deck! It's strange but real & maybe even beyond belief but I thank the Lord for taking me off those streets.

"ITS STILL JAIL"

We can complain about the cold air, we can complain about them taking our chairs. Believe it or not our complaints become still once it's all said & done were still in jail.

They take our curtains we use for our privacy; we argue & fuss about what is on TV. We don't go outside weekly as scheduled, let's take some off this is jail I tell you!

The food is bogus & it's never enough, let's stop playing with our selves we made our bed Ruff!

The soap is pretty much a one-time use, they barely give us toothpaste, is this a zoo? You're sharing a shower with 47 different guys; I wonder what's going on in the world while all this time is going by!

Even commissary items are outrageously priced, I'm not enduring this affliction again ever in life.

I stand corrected & rehabilitated too. I'm not coming back 2 jails, I don't know about you!

<u>"FREEDOM"</u>

For any bro, that's ever been detained or convicted, can understand the desire of freedom while going through your affliction.

Freedom is so beautiful; you don't appreciate till it's gone, because if it's taken from you, there are only dreams of making it home.

Being able to come & go & do things as you please, doing things when you get ready when you feel like it, life can be a breeze.

I've heard once before, if you don't use it, you'll lose it, I guess it's true with freedom, especially if you abuse it.

It's almost like a bird that's free, being able to roam constantly, then there's a bird that a pet the will never know what he missed.

Freedom- meaning the condition of being free, unrestricted use of access, it all sounds real good to me.

Over 800 years of slavery, & then finally our race was set free, oh what a great accomplishment, one of the greatest they'll ever be.

They lock you up & try to lose the key & then one day you finally become free.

Freedom is remarkable, beautiful & outstanding, the right to use your mind as you please, because the opposite is demanding.

If you ever been through a difficult relationship, and you find yourself very frustrated, once it over you exhale, you now have freedom & you can make it!

"NO BOND"

A bond is money paid, upon reason or release, I guess
that's why I don't have one, and they don't want me free.

If my mother won the lottery, like millions I mean having
her son out, would just be a dream.

The judge said, you have multiple cases so I'm issuing a
"no bond" she might as well said you're not going nowhere,
don't move, or you won't catch another one.

I guess its disrespectful 2 catch case, upon case, but 2 me is
uncivilized not 2 be able to bond out of this place.

These people are insane, 2 tell me there's no amount I can
pay, so I have 2 sit & endure this incarceration, no way.

Are you serious, NO BOND? I have a felony conviction
that's not an X, these people try 2 make your life
complicated & would like 2 keep you stressed.

Cook county jail, its real no doubt, my day will be here
eventually & I will be let out!

"GOING HOME"

Thoughts & dreams run through my head, missing the comfort of my own bed.

Losing weight from not eating right, growls from my stomach late at night,

Missing turning over to my girl, didn't appreciate these things when I was in the world.

Simple things you don't miss them till there gone, thoughts & visions of "GOING HOME".

Not just incarcerated bros, you got bros in the service too, I know they have similar feelings too.

You sit back & wonder was I really that bad? To take all the precious things that I had?

Have I learned my lesson? You better know its true! It just doesn't seem fair the things I'm going through!

So you locked me up, did you throw away the key? Do I even exist to society?

I don't think this is fair, it's no way this could be right! I wouldn't subject this to a dog night after night! Un-proportioned food, bogus temperatures on deck, now I understand why it's called correct!

After you endure these extreme & ridiculous living conditions, all you'll be doing is reminiscing!

I should of never ran that red light, if I could do it over I would reverse that night, I've accepted the fact of my doing wrong, god grant me my prayer I want to go home!

"BACK AGAINST THE WALL"

Once they get you, yeah they got you, they try to lose you
& forget about you!

Some way you land, in this county jail, and oh what
interesting stories they tell!

The system is so bogus; they just keep continuing your case,
just so you can sit longer in this place!

They try to break your mind, body & soul, if it wasn't for
god, you would lose control!

An average mind has to come to a point, where it has to say
I'm no longer coming to this joint!

After you fight your case for so long, all that is on your
mind is try to make it home!

They know they got your back against the wall, so they
offer you a deal, 2 get the case resolved.

In your mind, what should I do? I want to get out this jam,
Lord knows it's true.

If you're blessed with a paid lawyer your chances are better,
because the Pd's and state work together!

From weeks 2 months & months 2 years man I can't
believe I'm still up in here!

In most cases, these people get their conviction, along with
our time, pain & affliction.

I'm going to stand strong and say no longer will my back
be against the wall "I know I'm done now what about y'all"?

"NOTHING BUT TIME"

So many thoughts, racing through your brain, so many thoughts can drive you insane. I wonder what's going on with that person, what's happening with that one? Things I use 2 do, the ways I use to have fun.

Weeks upon weeks & months on end. Where is my family now? Even my closest friends. Yes I'm locked up, but am I thrown away? Are my memories erased since no one can see my face?

Over 600 friends on my Facebook page are they missing my statuses since I'm locked away? I'm sitting here, with nothing but time, thinking & wondering while all this time is going by.

I know when I get out everyone will have an excuse, man I didn't know how 2 get up with you dude. IDOC.com gives you all the information, on anyone you want to know about while their incarcerated.

Is it this reason I'm locked up? Was the thing I was doing really wrong when I got caught?

Maybe I could have been doing more for my children, or is everything just my fault?

People break bad when they know you're locked away, if it was that simple they weren't true anyway.

I got news for the so called love ones, a few months, it really won't be long, all my thanks & praise go to god. I'm on my way home!

"THE POWER OF GOD"

Miraculous, astounding, amazing & great for those of you who don't understand ill help you relate.

The power of god is remarkably real; the power of god will make you be still.

The power is great it can beat any case; this power is tough it can beat even lust.

This power of god can change any heart, the power of god can keep you blessed, and the power of god will relieve any stress.

He's giving us the power to change, we can use it, or lose it, or remain the same.

Give him your life, surrender to him, your days will be bright & never be dim.

Power is authority, clout or a force, & once you have submitted to him, you're on the right course. Going through life's situations & if you have god he will give your patience.

If you want peace& joy everyday of your life, invite him into your heart, & watch his love get you right.

"PLEASE LORD"

Please keep me safe while I run this race? Please keep me safe while I fight this case?

Please keep me safe while I'm sleep at night? Please keep me safe when my moods not right?

Watch over me in my daily walk, please guide my tongue when it time to talk!

Take away anything that's not pleasing to you; renew my mind so I can be obedient to you.

Cleanse my heart & just make me better, I want 2 get this done now; it's either now or never.

Strengthen my body, rejuvenate my soul, please Lord, and please Lord take full control?

I want you in my spirit, please change my heart, I won't your holy spirit to give me a brand new start.

I'm serious with this; you know my heart let your holy spirit tear my soul apart!

The prayer of a righteous man availed much. I know you hear me I can feel your touch.

I have not, because I ask not & I'm asking please so I thank you Lord in advance.

FOR BLESSING ME!

"DEPARTMENT OF CORRECTIONS"

Where do I start? Don't even know how to begin; well the first stage is processing in!

Hours upon hours getting all the technicalities done, from scanners to pictures, lying in multiple bull pens none of this is fun!

Now you finally get sent to your deck, your body is worn out, and you're tired as heck!

So you jump in the shower, feeling so unclean, and the guys are hollering "ON THE NEWS" so you're wondering what does that mean?

Up at 5 a.m. in order to get a morsel of food, if you don't wake up you'll be starving till noon.

Mind you breakfast and lunch is always cold. When you finally make it to dinner when it's hot you don't even want 2 know.

A modern day form of slavery if you ask me, this is a place a dog wouldn't want to be!

I think I left out were all wearing tan uniforms, I guess that color reflects opposite of the norm!

In the visiting room in division five, if you look up there's an interesting sign, spend time with your child now, so I won't have to later!

Over 11,000 inmates still counting they'll make room, when they run out of beds they use the floor its true.

Department of correction the name is so real, if you don't stand corrected, the next man will.

"WHY DO I FEEL ALONE"?

Why do I feel all alone? I guess it's just me missing home.

Why do I feel all alone? Maybe it's just my faith getting weak when I know it's strong! Missing getting up going to work , missing making money until it hurts, missing the sun beaming down on me, missing the warmth of a summer breeze.

Why do I feel all alone? Missing the comfort of my cell phone, it's the little things that you miss so much, like the gentle softness of a woman's touch.

They tell me this is where you come, when you commit a crime, where you are being detained until you get your time. They tell me you're not being cooked but corrected, you're not being punished but processed, you're not being arrested but rescued whatever, there's interesting things that you go through!

Emotions roaring, thoughts running a race, I pray 2 the Lord that I beat this case!

Lord if you bless me 2 come from up under this I will be so thankful & have my wish!

CHAPTER 3
"LOVE"

"LOVING YOU UNCONDITIONALLY"

I will love you at your strength, I will love you when you're weak, I will love you when you're sick, and I will love you when you're sleep.

I will love you when you're up, I will love you when you're down, I will love you when were together, I will love you when you're not around.

My love 4 u cannot be measured; you are my gift, my real true treasure. Are you a dream? Or are you real? I cannot explain the way you make me feel.

Extreme heat, sub-zero cold, how long will I love you? Until time gets old.

All my time gets spent with you, all my love gets given to you, and my heart belongs to you, without you girl what would I do?

Until the end of time, I want you here, until the end of time, I want you near. Let me love you & you'll be fine, I am so thankful that you are mine!

I loved you then, I love you now, I will love you later, all with a smile.

I just want this love 2 last, hoping this love would never past!

Not just for years, but eternally, my love for you is,

UNCONDITIONALLY!

"TRUE LOVE"

My definition of love is pretty profound & deep my definition of love is more than being intimate between the sheets.

First you have love that is fake, then you have love that is true, I mean there are so many indescribable things & feelings you may subdue.

Maturity is important, interesting thought level, is a must, but you'll know if you found "true love" there's no doubt of trust.

Financial stability is a great quality & also sexy plays a big part infatuation or really "true love" will occur once that person has your heart.

Thoughts & dreams revolving around you, feelings & emotions just doing what they do.

Longing to see you when you're not around, can't wait to be with you to see you smile.

There's no one else, that has made me feel this way, you're the only person that's takes my breath away. These feelings are indescribable, I feel free as a dove & there's no doubt this is "true love".

I searched high & low, I searched near & far, through the entire galaxy in between shooting stars.

There's no second guessing, this is truly one of a kind, I'm so thankful that you're mine.

To be your man I excelled, to be your husband only time will tell, you are definitely the lady I want in my life, let me drop to one knee and ask me to be my wife?

CHAPTER 4
"INSPIRATION"

"HOLD ON"

You've been pushing real hard to make it 2 your goal,
giving all of your effort, where you're ready 2 explode.

Push a little more, you got it in you 4 sure, because gods
not going to give you more than you can endure.

Your fight has been hard & you're almost out of breath,
your wind has got exhausted & almost no stamina is left.

It's like holding on the edge & your grip has become lose,
just call on the Lord & he'll give you a boost.

When you're climbing 2 the top & so many obstacles are in
your way, once you give it 2 gods, he'll make it vanish
away!

When you're waiting for your ship 2 come in & you want 2
give up & your faith starts 2 ends.

Be cool, relax, & please remain strong, continue 2 pray &
just plain "hold on"!

"THIS TOO SHALL PAST"

Depressing moments, times of gloom, sometimes take a while, sometimes come too soon.

Lonely days will not always last, believe it or not this too shall past. Murphy's Law does exist & karma is definitely real. You reap what you sow that's why we have free will.

Issues upon issues, with life moving so fast, disappointments and setbacks "to shall pass"! Things did not go truly as planned, with all mistakes & unpleasant circumstances all on hand.

All life's obstacles are coming full force, just stay focused & stay on course, after the storm, the sun will shine & all your worries are left behind.

After the winter, then comes spring, then comes summer, along with many beautiful things.

Endure the winter, endure the warm, endure the heat, and endure the storm.

Everything in life has a season, everything in life has a reason, and all unpleasantness will not last, all life's origins to shall past.

"DON'T GIVE UP IT WRONG ME LONG"

The road been rough, as it sometimes will & all your stops have been uphill. Hold on tight, it won't be long don't give up & remain strong.

Your way has been blocked, with twist &turns &all your thoughts have become discern, you entered the race, don't give up now, it won't be long then you can smile.

Be cool, hold fast & please be still, you must have faith, & you must have will.

Issues & problems are a part of life; just stay posted & with stand the fight.

You're doing well, keep it up, you're not done yet, when your battle is over then you can rest.

Push hard, stay determined, stay true to your goal, never look back, & only accomplishments will unfold.

Get it together, you're almost there, the pain has stopped, no more despair, don't give up, it won't be long, hold your head up high.

YOU'RE ALMOST HOME!!

"TIME OF TROUBLE"

When the wicked ones are opposing you, when the animals won't to tear you through & through.

When you're trying to live right, & even be Christ like the demon comes lurking day & night.

Even in the belly of the whale, god is there with you, so you will prevail, if you're truly a Christian, anointed, a child of god, please do not fear, you're protected by his rod.

I will never leave you all alone, even when you're weak, I'll make you strong, if your spirit is soft as a rabbit, he'll make you a bear, god is the answer he's always there!

Disappointments in life, depressing news, when you're down in the dumps & you just have the blues.

Your trouble will not last always, don't even trip they'll be better days, this duress, & despair too shall pass & when your struggles is over only god will last!

As long as you stay grounded & encouraged & true to the Lord, when the time cones, he'll cut it up with a double edged sword.

"WISDOM"

American heritage reason- understanding of what is true, in laymen terms commons sense, and thoughts from struggle will also do.

I believe wisdom can come through struggle, because through trials you obtain knowledge because through your fight and your turmoil you become a scholar.

Wisdom should increase with age, if you're going through the proper stage, if it does not do not worry, something's in life do not hurry.

One sign of wisdom is the hairs start to turn gray, but if it doesn't don't even trip life will school you anyway.

Life has a lot of lessons, which come with a ton of blessings, if you do things right and try to live a good life, you will not be stressing.

Wisdom comes with knowledge & knowledge with understanding when you mix it in with experience life can get demanding.

Good judgment is also wisdom, which can make you a good Christian. So just proceed through life, with all these qualities, and you can handle your business.

"OVERCOMING STRUGGLE"

Obstacles in life, can smack you real hard, you can lose everything in a breath if you lose your job.

What about the kids we cannot eat, if I can't pay the mortgage we'll be in the street.

If they re-po the car, how will we get around? Credit cards cut off also the bank account.

Things have gotten real rough, as you can see, within a wink of an eye, within a skip of a beat.

So I start thinking positive, and the results start showing, plus the tension leaves my brain and I no longer will cuss.

I was worried about food, and someone introduced me to the link card that will help us eat until I find another job.

So I filed a chapter thirteen that will save the house and car and things are looking brighter and it doesn't seem so dark.

My way had gotten thick and much clogged, and the bills all have doubled, but I think I'll be fine, since I overcame my struggle!

"THINGS WE GO THROUGH"

Life is interesting; there are trials & tribulations, different phases we go through all type of situations.

From grammar school, 2 high schools, where we learn & mature, all type of lessons things we just have to endure.

Even in school, we graduate from one level 2 another, getting use to one atmosphere readjusting to another.

Change & versatility is a part of life. Like a man having multiple girlfriends then one day having a wife.

There's a level of maturity that comes with wisdom & age which enables us to cope with all life's different phases.

Your environment plays a part on the things you go through, because you can follow everyone else or just do what you do.

Relationship, marriage, childbirth, & success is all things that we go through until were laid down 2 rest.

Please stay positive while going through life's situations, because if you do not you can wind up in unwanted places.

Jails & penitentiaries doors are wide open for you, so please be careful with the things we go through.

CHAPTER 5
"DEDICATIONS"

"KEEP YOUR HEAD UP"

You are the head of the family, you're the backbone, you must stay focused & you must stay strong.

You're an amazing woman, & I know nothing can keep you down, even when life's issues have you troubled, you keep a smile.

Trust in god, through all situations, & know that he's there for you through all complications.

If you need me, I'll be right there, I'm on my way, without a care.

I love you as a son, you can't be replaced, just keep your head up & don't give up the race.

No matter what the circumstances, it can always be worse, just stay encouraged & keep god first.

Sometimes our way seems dark, & the road may be rough, we just have to keep the line moving & don't give up.

Tie a knot, hang on tight, with stand the storm, with stand the fight.

Disappointments don't last always, keep your head up you'll see better days.

"YOU SAY YOU LOVE ME"

You say you love me, but I can't tell only seen your face
once in four months since I've been in jail, only once you
told me I've had money on my books, but when I placed
the order there was no need to look.

You say you love me, how can this be true; four letters in
four months what do you call that boo? You say you love
me, I wonder how & why, you have not been writing me on
the regular, while all this time is going by.

You say you love me, I don't understand, is this the way
it's supposed to be is it in your plan? You say you love me,
such a strong word to use; you have 2 show it honey,
because it feels like abuse! You say you love me? Are you
out of your mind? This is not the way you treat a man while
he's doing his time!

"GRAN DAD"

I want you to imagine, a role model, god fearing stand up man, if you cannot let me help u understand!

Granddad was someone who was always there, who showed nothing but love & truly cared.

All I can remember, coming up through life, he was a devoted family man & clung 2 his wife!

When grandma said no, granddad said yes, so it always fun 2 put issues 2 a test!

One thing he said, that sticks in my mind, when someone wants 2 bless you, receive it always remain kind!

In my 38 years he has never changed, humble, peaceful, loving it all remained.

He also taught me 2 pay my bills on time, credit is important in life you'll find.

When I needed a co-signer for my nice new car, granddad did it without hesitation & I've been good thus far.

I am so thankful & grateful 4 u being in my life, now you can finally be with your wife!

"HOW DO YOU JUST WALK AWAY"?

How do you just walk away? It's so many things that I wanted to say! How do you just walk away? Was your love true or was it fake? How do you just walk away? Four years of our life together, day after day. Was your heart in it? Yes or no? Because, if it was you just shut the door! Dramatic moments fussing & fighting, which was wrong? Who was right? Intensive moments supporting each other, emotional times, calling our mothers. How did you just walk away? Was it really that bad for you to just leave with no delay? How do you just walk away? I miss you so much; I wish I could see your face. What are you doing? Have you moved on with your life? Or are you just shutting me down so I can get right? Please think about me, just send me a letter, and give me another chance I know I'll do better! I loved you in the beginning, & I still love you now, & I was looking forward to the day you bear our child. All of the things & issues we dealt with each other, I just knew this love would last forever! And if it's meant we'll see each other again, & if we're not together than maybe just friends. My heart was warm but now it's cold how much I miss you you'll never truly know. If I was granted a one-time wish, I would want you right here so I could kiss your lips & ask you why & how did you just walk away? I would just sit & listen to whatever you had to say.

"MISSING YOU"

As I sit here with nothing but time, 75% of the day you occupy my mind.

Thinking of the good times we once shared, & when I really needed you & you were there.

We've had our ups & our downs, we've had our smiles & our frowns, and we've been through storms & through rail all kinds of arguments & too much pain.

I know I love you & this is true, that's why I'm missing the hell out of you!

Wondering how you're doing and if you're ok? But knowing gods got you, covered throughout your day.

4 years in & it hasn't been a piece of cake, but what's so strange is I can't wait until I see your face.

Emotions roaring, but I give god the glory, because when it's over ill have a hell of a story.

I'm a little confused on which way this should go, but there is something I want you 2 know, I love your crazy ass for show!

If this was formed from up above, then there's no doubt it is true love, and if it's not, it's been a hell of a ride, & there always a place for you inside my heart & mind.

"IF YOU DON'T WANT ME, THE NEXT ONE WILL"

I still exist, or do you even care? Because I'm still here, but are you still there? Don't even trip; it won't be that long, because this young man will soon be home!

I've always felt blessed & highly favored with talent & skills but if you don't want me, the next one will!

Yes I love you, I'm a Pisces we love hard, & have had your back for 4 years even though you had no job!

I'm going through one of the most critical points in my lifetime, & while I'm feeling so alone you've showed your behind!

Don't worry about me, I'll be cool, I'll be fine, but I guess it's true out of sight, out of mind.

I'm a good man, I work hard, I'm faithful & remain true, & always trying 2 do something 4 u!

I'm not dogging you, you did well you lasted 12 rounds, but through my incarceration you have really let me down!

When you're stuck in a jam, a lot of thoughts run through your brain, should I stay with her & remain or get away from this pain?

Even though my own family, said leave that crazy girl alone, but I stayed with you girl and kept my love strong!

"LOVE OF MY LIFE"

These 2 years have been the best of life, I simply can't wait until the day you become my wife, and I knew from that moment I laid eyes on that pretty smile, that I would always want you by my side, not just for a little while. You've been there for me, like no one else, girl your love is inexplicable. I just have to pinch myself. God sent me an angel, my real true treasure fat, fat the love I have for you. I just cannot measure as long as you exist, you're my one and only, as long as you exist, I'll never be lonely.

I love spending time with you; I love everything that we do. You've been there for me through thick & thin. I hope & pray this love never ends. You are my morning, and awesome soul mate, in a million years no one could take your place. You are my lady, my shooting star, baby do not change, stay the way you are. I want to cry because I love you so much, I want to cry because I miss your touch. Dream of me at night, & think of me in the day, the time is short before we see each other's face. If you were a lollipop I would leave none left, if you were a lollipop I would lick you to death. It's going to be cracking once I make it home, keep it warm baby it won't be long.

<u>"ANNA"</u>

It's been a long time, we have a lot of time to make up, I've really missed you my daughter this time without you been rough.

The thought of you has never left my mind, I think about you all the time.

You are my child, I would never leave you no way, my heart will be pleased, the day I see your face.

I only have memories right now 2 hold on too, but that's all I have to make it through.

I've watched you grow up from a seed to a rose, the love I have for you, you will never truly know!

There's no greater joy 2 a father than 2 see his baby girl grown, 2 become successful in life & being able 2 make it on her own.

I hope you understand I love you more than life, & I'm waiting on the day for us to reunite!

"TARA"

I tried this before & I made mistakes in the past, but believe me girl I really want to make this last!

While I'm in here, being detained you pretty much occupy 75% of my brain.

I hope you feel the same way I do, because I'm looking forward to spending years with you!

While were going through this situation, please don't be stressed, I've already prayed over it & ill know we'll be blessed.

I think about you constantly, most times from morning to noon and I know god will answer my prayers & I'll be home soon.

I had a dream that you gave me a little girl, I believe that dream came true, so please don't leave my world.

While you're out there maintain & watch over my lil bro, keep your head up & please stay in touch with my mother.

This love is real, so just hold fast & be still!

Don't even trip, its nothing but time, this wait will be over & we'll turnout just fine.

"SONG BIRD"

Such a beautiful name that matches a beautiful face, just an amazing lady that lights up any place.

I admire you, I mean you're doing your thing; you're a mother, a boss, a diva above all things.

My loving & dear sister, I wish you much joy & success in everything that you encounter, & pray that you stay blessed.

I've watched you grow from a child to a lady, you've matured & you blossomed & drive most men crazy.

Happy birthday baby sister, you're exquisite & unique, I love you extremely from your head down to your feet!

Enjoy your birthday & just do what you do. Have a wonderful birthday & may your wishes come true!

"TASHA"

Throughout this time I've missed you so much, can't wait 2 be with you 2 feel your touch.

You are my girl, my wife 2 be, the only woman my eyes can see.

The four years we spent together, those memories alone are my great treasure.

It won't be long; I know it's been a while, anticipating the day you bear our child.

We exchanged name tattoos, I will wear it forever, I can't wait 2 get out so were back together.

You should know I love you, I chose you for life, and I'll be over whelmed once you become my wife!

God is good, god is great, he out did his self when he sent you my way!

"HAPPY BIRTHDAY MOM"

On this day unlike no other, god created my dear mother
I'm so privileged just to say I wish you joy & happiness on
your birthday.

Happy birthday mom & enjoy your day. Do what you like
&have things your way.

I'm wishing you excellence & blessings in everything that
you do, & I want you to know that I love & miss you too.

I want you to accept gods favor each & every day, & know
that in all situations you're covered by his grace.

Happy birthday mom, you're a star shining so bright, I'm
so thankful & grateful that you gave me life.

I wish you positivity, prosperity, & longevity throughout
your life, & anything that's not in order know that god will
get it right.

I'm sending you this birthday poem, with hopes of
greatness, & success I'm sending you this birthday poem
only because you are the best.

"STAY ENCOURAGED"

When time of trouble are caving in, when you feel lost & don't have a friend, stay encouraged, keep your head up days will get brighter just don't give up!

Stay encouraged, remain positive, peace & happiness is the only way 2 live.

Why frown when you can smile, don't let situations get you down!

Stay encouraged everything will work out, times will get better without a doubt.

Stay encouraged pull it together, dark days don't last forever.

Stay encouraged & always remains true, stay encouraged is all you got to do!

Stay encouraged in all aspects of life, stay encouraged & you'll be alright.

<u>CHAPTER 6</u>

"A LITTLE BIT OF EVERYTHING"

"WHERE IS MY WIFE"

Every woman that I come across brings a lot of drama, is it because I'm a boss?

Am I asking too much? When I say sexy & a job? Or are those qualities just 2 damn hard?

When I say I'm a boss, I mean I like finer things, like filet minion, nice cars & big flat screens.

One who doesn't mind cooking & cleaning & all those womanly duties, I'll take out the garbage, pay my portion of the bills & love hitting your booty!

A god fearing woman, we can go 2 church together, & bear all life's trials & tribulations for now & forever,

Family functions, engagements, taking trips, the whole nine, I really wouldn't mind having that in my life!

If she's out there, I'm here, it can be now or next year, I'll accept her, receive her & promise never to leave her!

If god blesses me with the one 2 call wife that will truly give me a beautiful life!

"DIVINE ORDER"

There is order in everything that we do, you have free will, which one will you choose?

Everything has a process, everything has a chain of command, everything has a stage, and everything has a plan.

There are rules & regulations in every aspect of life, from a child acting up in school to an adult running a red light.

There are consequences to our actions & we all have someone we have to answer to, there's some type of divine order in everything that we do.

Yes there has to be order not just for one, but for all, if you cut off the head, the body will definitely fall.

There has to be a head, there has to be a chief, there has to be structure, and there has to be police.

Someone has to enforce laws & violations; someone has to enforce order for the nation.

Without order, there would be no control, without order the world would just fold.

There's divine order in everything that we do, so we have to govern our self's accordingly. That's just the way it is & the way it should be.

"THE BLACK MAN"

If you're blessed to be middle class, who at least 50% of us do then your upbringing and passages won't be so hard 4 you.

If there's a religious back bone within your family's life, then most definitely all your issues and obstacles will be alright!

Your religious back bone keeps you grounded, & being middle class keeps you surrounded with wants & necessities of life, which keeps down most quarrels & fights.

The other half that's not blessed with good qualities and success can be forced with a lot of difficulties in their way & a lot of dark days.

Reaching the stage of adolescence, there's a lot of peer pressure, and heavy questions, going through stages of trying to figure it out, with temptations and thoughts of doubt.

We got to figure out more black on black love, so we can stop the jealousy & envy so we can please the "god" above.

Being a black man is an interesting thing, it's pretty much dealing with obstacles and issues life brings.

One of the most interesting things about being black is what we do, we dominate and that's a fact, ill spirits we dominate, jails and penitentiaries we dominate, positive & negative denominator, interesting trait.

So many issues the black man has 2 face, from simply walking down the street to catching a felony case, when I add it all together positive & negative I love being a black man &just going 2 continue 2 live!

"WHO AM I?"

I am a brother who's creative, like writing poetry and stuff, and unique type of man, who's working on trying not 2 cuss.

I'm real and sincere, pretty much don't play to many games, but I'm humble & positive, my mood pretty much stays the same.

I'm a hustler no doubt; I pretty much find a way 2 work it out! But I'm a poet & I know it, my creative side often shows it!

I'm daring & caring, versatile & don't mind sharing. I'm spiritual & smart & come straight from my heart.

I'm a man of many qualities, but pretty much one of a kind, but I also live by the quote "I got to get mine".

I'm dramatic, & experienced & a tad emotional, but I know when things get rough, I just stop and read my bible!

So you ask me who am I? Life is good please believed me, & those of you who don't know I go by "EDDIE B"!

"CHANGE"

Change is something one must want to do; it can only come from inside of you.

Change is good, it builds character, & motivation, and the right change can upgrade your situation.

Never be afraid 2 endure change, nothing in life remains the same!

From hostile to humble, from broke 2 rich, one minute having everything, next stuck down in a ditch.

Me, myself I don't mind change, I like the versatility, & the difference it brings.

The flesh is interesting it always want more, first we crawl, then walk, then ran on the floor.

Sometimes it takes courage, & faith 2 fulfills a complete change, once it gets started everything falls in place like the rain.

Something different, something new, and something fresh, change will do!

"EXPERIENCE IS THE BEST TEACHER"

When things in life teach you a lesson, and you wonder is it a curse or a blessing.

Some people lie and fake like they did it, others done it, and know how to get it.

If you really want to know some facts about life, you got to go through it in order to get it right.

It's cool to listen to opinions, and then make your own decisions, because what they went through, & the way they did it could have been stupendous.

Everyone is different, with their own qualities at heart, because the way they could have finished probably was different at the start.

One person telling you does it this way, another person telling you another, who do I suppose to listen to, my girl or her brother?

I can tell you which way to go, you may choose not to listen, but I'm speaking from experience & I already did it! you don't have to take my advice, because you have to live your own life, but if you listen 2 me, there's some things you won't have to do twice.

I listened to my mother, I listened to my preacher, when I summed it all up, "EXPERIENCE IS THE BEST TEACHER"!

"VIOLENCE, WHEN DOES IT STOP"?

It starts in the home, the upbringing of a child, & what matters the most is both parents are there for a significant amount of years & not just a little while. Raising a child from a boy to a man, keeping him in many activities is a part of the plan. Teaching a child manners, along with respect & there must be discipline in order to pass life's test! Spending plenty of time with the child, also showing him much love, there must also be a strong presence of god so he knows all blessings are from above. Teaching the child right from wrong, so he can conduct himself in the street when he is all alone.

There is divine order in everything you do, so you have to govern yourself accordingly & when these things are not done, this is why there is so much chaos in the streets. The economy plays a part, because times are so very hard, there is no finance being rotated because there are not many jobs. Young men are not able to receive the cars & clothes they see on TV, so they take their resources to the streets! Armed robberies, burglaries, home invasions & more, drug dealing & shootings like never before!

Violence has reached an all-time peak, there has to be a stop to this destruction throughout these street! From ages 10 to 30, bullets are flying everywhere. Babies are dying, does anyone care? Once you turn on the news it looks like we have just lost control, when will this violence stop, does anyone really know? Senseless killings day after day. Let's stop the violence, let's put the guns away! Someone's mother, someone father, someone's brother, someone's daughter, someone's uncle, someone niece. Can we stop the violence and just have PEACE!

"CHESS"

Here is a game that stimulates the mind, that pretty much progress more with time.

I've come to find out your opening means a lot, because the way you present it, is the way it could stop.

The object of the game is 2 get a "check mate" but along with that comes a lot of risk you'll take.

It takes a lot of sacrifice 2 get to your goal, giving up power pieces so you can have full control.

Who out thinks who is the name of the game, the strongest thinker, is the one with the fame?

You must have all pieces in position, so they can protect, threaten & take, if you do all of this right you can call a "check mate".

Every player has a different level of play & strategy, but playing a person better than you is when you get better & less tragedies.

If you want 2 stimulate your mind, & increase your thoughts learn & play this game & your thinking will be well off.

"UNDERSTANDING"

You cannot lean to your own thoughts; you cannot lean to another mean but only lean to god if you want to truly understand.

There are things that are going to discuss you, there are so many problems right at hand, and so many things are so confusing you will not understand.

Where did this come from, how did this originate, where did I go wrong? Which wrong turn did I make?

Thoughts upon thoughts and questions begin to weigh? You wonder the reason is it because of fate?

Some situations can disrupt you, there are people who will corrupt you, just get your thoughts in line, and one day at a time with correct understanding you will be fine.

Webster's meaning says agreement between two or more, or intelligence mine is knowledge knowing forever more.

Once you have knowledge of your entire plan, with proper organization all on point, at hand, with divine order you will understand, so just thank the Lord hallelujah and now say AMEN!

"IT'S ALL ABOUT WHO YOU KNOW"

There are things that you would like to do, & there's places you would like to go, but there's certain people with capabilities you just have to know.

In all areas of life there's people who can make things right, whatever it is you are trying to do there's people who can get this done for you.

You got people who make power moves, people in positions to see it through, someone whose ready to hook you up. Someone who's ready to come up.

These people are known as networkers, they make things happen & that's for certain.

From plane tickets to train tickets, from used cars to favorite bars, from real estate to birthday cakes, to whatever decision you're trying to make.

Were always trying to maneuver & manage our plan, it would help if we had aid & assistance when we can.

People in positions get things done, which it makes it better for everyone, wherever you are, wherever you go, there's people in areas you just must know.

"TRUE HUSTLER"

I want you to try & comprehend, the way a true hustlers day begin.

In my vehicle driving cab trying 2 get all the cash that I can grab!

Once the passenger gets in my car, I add up the trip &get my bread up front, either near or far.so I offer packs of squares, loosies, movies & CDs, I know how to get that bread please believe me!

12 hours & counting still getting it in, pick-ups & drop offs until I have no wind. All up north, airports, & downtown, I'm all over the place making my rounds. From midnight to noon the next day, I hustle real hard, doing it my way! Then I have a young lady I have to tend too, so my day is not over until our time is through.

7 days a week, I do not rest, I'm a true hustler I do my best! I hustle real hard I thought you knew, I'm a true hustler I make it do what it do!

"SOMETIMES IT'S BEST TO BE SILENT THAN 2 BE HEARD"

Just because I'm quiet, don't judge my mood, I'm not being mean, nothing's wrong I'm cool.

I may be debating on some major moves, like which bill 2 pay first, like which one will I choose?

Issues come up, the kids have necessities that they need, my mom's sick, the weather man says were going into a deep freeze.

Sometimes it takes time 2 get my thoughts in order, so I organize my brain like a professional sorter.

Most time when I'm quiet, I can feel my brain work; it's like hearing yourself think when you're doing research.

At times you can open your mouth & say the wrong things, but if you stay silenced, its only thoughts they can dream.

It takes two to argue, which things can become heated, but if one becomes silent the argument has been defeated.

A fight originates from words that come out of your mouth so if you are quiet & walk away, you really shut it down.

Silence is golden, it's your choice, what to do, you can be loud & raise hell or be silent and mute.

I summed it all up & came up with this, you can achieve more things being quiet than throwing a fit.

"PATIENCE"

Patience is something that you learn, like when you're a child waiting your turn.

Patience is waiting, weeks, months, years; you just keep on waiting until the time grows near.

You learn patience when you want something real bad, pretty much something you've never had.

During your patience, you gained respect, because it was worth the wait, now you can rest.

Patience has always been hard for me; I was pretty much spoiled as a child, so I'm used 2 things instantaneously.

As I matured and grew with age, I realized getting thing when you want them was just a phase.

Especially when I stepped out on my own, I found out patience was a major part of being grown.

Now you have bills & responsibility to, so getting things for yourself doesn't come around like it used to.

Patience is something that we all must use a very interesting thing. But am important tool.

"DESIRES"

A desire is something you want real bad, dreams of things you've never had.

First it's a thought, and then it's a want, days after days, months after months.

A desire is something or a way you want the world to be through your eyes the way you see.

You can ask 4 it, receive it, & or never get it, & dream it? Be sincere when you ask so the desire can last.

As long as you stay true, a real desire comes from inside of you!

It can be a mate, money, house, even a car as long as it's coming from your heart!

What is that you desire? It can be anything as long as it's burning with fire!

It comes from your head, sits in your heart, & lays there until it tears you apart.

We have not, because we ask not, is what the bible says. So remember that throughout your days.

"HUMBLE"

To bring yourself down from higher stage, from flamboyant to meek in a couple of days.

On the top of the mountain, living like a boss, steak & lobster, and jumbo shrimp like there are no cost.

The Lord giveth and he takes it away, just remember where you came from, and know it was your faith.

Everything falls in divine order, so govern yourself accordingly, and remember the laws of humbleness is the only way 2 remain free.

If the outcome didn't come out the way that you planned, just know that you're getting a lesson in humbleness, so try and understand.

The first time you tried it, it didn't go through, the second time you failed, what am I going to do?

The third time I flopped and became very frustrated! On the fourth go round believe it or not I finally made it!

If you don't win, and so happen 2 lose, always remember the golden rule!

Stay humble 2 thy self & always remain true, because when you are humble you still win even when you lose.

"PISCES"

Creative and compassionate, caring, good hearted people, some of the best friends in life and know how to keep a secret.

A lot of people try to take advantage of our kindness, and once they do that they can stir up some mess.

A Pisces is a friend 2 the end, they stand firm and wont bend.

Will listen to your problems, and give you solutions on solving them.

Two fish symbolize two different moods, from warm hearted to cold, which ever they choose.

A Pisces can make an admitted soul mate, when they love them love hard and bot afraid to admit mistakes.

I advise you 2 find you a real true Pisces friend because when the road gets rough they will be there to the end.

When it's all said and done, Pisces people we are the ones, to stick by you when the rest are gone, by your side to keep you strong.

"HUSTLIN"

Just because you didn't graduate college, and become as famous as Charlie sheen, doesn't mean you didn't know how to get that green!

You can be an entrepreneur, which means working for one's self, a chief of your own business, and building your own wealth.

American heritage meaning – to hurry along, to work busily, but their slang is to sell or get it, by questionable or aggressive means.

Webster's definition- is to get by any means necessary, which I favor a lot, which is more to my mature, more to my shop.

If you choose to hustle as most bros do, just remember to be real and keep it true.

I learned at a young age, if you want it work hard for it, so that's pretty much how I grew up getting the things that I got.

You get out, of what you put in- so it's your endurance that keeps you hustling!

Money never sleeps is one of my tats, I think I'll do a life picture next and put it on my back.

If you go to work, and pay your bills, it's a form of hustling; it's the white and blue collar deal.

I pretty much got it all summed up 3 different businesses I got it all in the ruff.

A man usually works from sun to sun but a hustler work is never done.

"RELIEF"

Relief is something once you have overcame to put all struggle away to shame.

Once you have passed your test, won your race, became successful beat your case!

When the victory is won and the party is over and done, take a deep breath and exhale & you now have stories to tell.

When you've endured the storm, completed the war, came up for air and trouble is no more.

It's the feeling you have once you aced the course, it's the peace of mind right after a rough divorce.

It's the way you feel after a severe accident once you left the hospital where most of your time has been spent.

Where you worked hard on a project, and put your best foot in it, and knew in your heart you were going to win it.

It's a great feeling knowing when it's all said and done once your victory is over and all is won.

"DEPENDABLE"

You won't have to worry, if they'll come through, without a care, they'll be there for you.

Have you ever had a person once you make that call, they were there in a second without a pause.

Dependable meaning whenever in need, coming hastily in large amounts of speed.

It's a blessing when you have someone you can always rely on, there as close as your fingers are to the phone.

In a financial situation, where you low in cash, once you're really made it down to your last.

If you find yourself sitting in a peculiar situation, and you end up sitting in a police station.

When your back is truly against the wall, there's that one person that comes fear sly just like the fall.

I thank god for my earthly father who's been there through thick & thin.

Through all my 39 years, there's been no end!

Unbelievable thanks; to my heavenly father I don't know how I could have made it through.

Thank you Lord, without you what could I do?

"FORGIVING"

When someone does you wrong as they sometimes will, it makes it so difficult to just forgive.

If you're the type of person, who stands firm on thoughts and really doesn't care if any love was lost.

You might find it frustrating just to open your mouth and let those very precious words come out.

I forgive you, and this is true, when you do this you remove the grudge, which opens the doors for blessings for you.

When you let bygones be bygones, it's truly the way to live, it's such an honor and a sacrifice to just forgive.

You can get so upset, where you lose your cool, and say things you don't mean just plain acting a fool.

After you calm down, and have come back to earth, you've realized that there are feelings you've hurt.

So you reach into your heart, deep down inside, and you put away your pride.

Now you have pretty much figured out how to forgive, which is a great quality in life, and a great way to live.

"OBEDIENCE"

Complying with ones instructions, in authority or going against the grain to your own priority.

Were taught obedience at a young age, the difference between right and wrong but as we mature we make choices on our own.

Our parents trust we used what we learned, to the best of our knowledge, all the way through grade school, and some even through college.

Being obedient to rules, being obedient to laws, being obedient in all aspects without any flaws.

Obedience is a mindset which you have to master, because if you do not you'll be headed for disaster.

If you do not be obedient, your infractions too shall pass, from different ranges of traffic tickets, to simply taking a class.

Once you reached the level of disobedience which god has enforced, you can find yourself on a very harsher course.

Disobeying god is not a nice thing, because no one can whip you like god and the drama it brings.

I'm going to end in saying, let's all stop playing and be obedient to the Lord, stand strong and carry our sword.

"MY KIDS"

So proud & honored with my first born, even though it didn't work with me and his mother.

Some years later, there came a girl, who brought a lot of happiness in my world.

We bared three kids, very interesting & fun, until one day she decided to run, all the way 2 Minnesota, it was difficult & hard now I'm a part time father with a part time job.

My oldest is graduating high school this year, with a lot of honor & a lot of cheer.

Very excited to see him cross the stage with all the pains & difficulties he faces!

I love my children to the bitter end, I want them all to succeed in life and win.

I thank god for all my kids, I want them to do better in life than I did!

"TOLERANCE LEVELS"

The capacity to endure hardship or pain, the more we endure it strengthens the range.

When I first started playing chess my game was week, as I played more & more I strengthen my winning streak.

The more you endure, the more you can endure, take it from me I know for sure.

Tolerance level is an interesting thing; you upgrade your level when you're consistent with the same thing.

Practice makes perfect, stick with it, you'll win it always get greater when you get to the end.

We all have a limit of how much we can take, the more you deal with it the stronger your intake.

How much hardship can one person take? It's all up to the level of tolerance they make.

I've sat through the storm, and took on all the rain, but couldn't take no more when my level exhausted in pain.

Levels can be high; levels can be low, only you know your level of tolerance you can take through the door.

"LET YOUR YES MEAN YES & YOUR NO MEAN NO"

Standing firm without a doubt, mean what you say when these words come out.

Once you have made up your mind, do not let your decision change with time.

Change meaning something different, from what it was, staying true to your thought not flip flopping just because.

Decide meaning judgment or choice, as long as you stay determined once you cast your voice.

So let your yes mean yes & your no mean no, whatever you figure out stay focused on whatever you choose through the door.

Yes- meaning to give an affirmative to or reply. No- meaning negative or rejection and always leaves questions of why?

"HATERS"

A hater originates from a person who has less than you, or pretty much wishing they could do the things you do.

It starts off with envy & jealousy, escalating 2 hate, next thing you know their mugging you when they see your face.

Maybe in their childhood their parents didn't raise them right, because I myself hate has never existed in my life!

Dad always taught me you see something you want, work hard for it, I did a lot of book reports and chores to get things I wanted to get.

I might have a dollar more than you, so you don't like me dude? Or I got a nice bank account so you want to take me out?

We all have different talents, skills and levels of education, which make us able to choose different grades of cars and live in mediocre to wealthy locations.

Of course we all want to live lavish, but haven't made it yet, so let's be thankful for what we have & stop hating on the rest!

Hate is such a strong wrong, so don't give yourself that title, you're going to come up one day & they'll hate you too! Alright!

From the projects to apartments, condos & houses, mansions & lofts to 3 story castles.

It doesn't matter how less or how much, if they're going to hate they're going to hate! So just get used to it bro...

About the Author

POETRY HAS ALWAYS BEEN IN EDDIE'S SYSTEM STARTING AT THE YOUNG AGE OF EIGHT WHEN HIS DAD "JUKUBE FELTON" CHALLENGED EDDIE TO MEMORIZE HIS FIRST PIECE TITLED "**SUCCESS**" OUT OF THE BOOK "THINK AND GROW RICH" BY NAPOLEON HILL, THE "CHALLENGE WAS TO MEMORIZE THE PIECE AND RECITE IT AND EDDIE WOULD BE AWARDED A BRAND NEW "BIKE" MISSION ACCOMPLISHED & THIS STARTED EDDIE' S LOVE FOR POETRY.

ALL THROUGH EDDIE'S LIFE, HE HAS WRITTEN AND RECITED PIECES OF POETRY AT FAMILY AND CLOSE FRIEND FUNERALS.

IN 2012, EDDIE WAS INCARCERATED; HE WAS DETAINED AT COOK COUNTY JAIL FOR SEVEN A HALF MONTHS AND SHANEE CORRECTIONAL INSTITUTION FOR NINETY SEVEN DAYS. DURING HIS STAY, HE OBTAINED TWO THINGS: AN "INTIMATE RELATIONSHIP "WITH "GOD" AND AN "INSPIRATION TO WRITE!

AFTER BEING RELEASED, EDDIE STUMBLED UPON INTERNET POETRY RADIO SHOWS, WHERE HE FREQUENTS 22 DIFFERENT SHOWS A WEEK!

EDDIE THEN STARTED HITTING OPEN MICS THROUGHOUT THE CITY AND SUBURBS OF ILLINOIS. HE HAS BEEN ON OVER 85 STAGES, 10 PAID FEATURES,OVER 20 CHURCH APPEARANCES, PARTICIPATED AND PLACED AND WON SEVERAL POETRY CONTEST AND SLAMS!

EDDIE WAS CROWNED AND TITLED ONE OF CHICAGO'S "PRINCES OF POETRY" AND MAINTAINS HIS OWN INTERNET RADIO SHOW **"WELL~SPOKEN"** WHICH AIRS EVERY THIRD THURSDAY OF THE MONTH. HE ALSO HOST HIS OWN POETRY SET **"WELL~SPOKEN LIVE!!"** IN CHICAGO EVERY OTHER MONTH AND THE THIRD THURSDAY OF THE MONTH! EDDIE OWES ALL OF HIS ACCOMPLISHMENTS TO **"GOD"** WHO IS THE HEAD OF HIS LIFE!!!

Poet/Spoken Word Artist/Host/Author

Eddie Felton aka WORD WARRIOR